To: _____

From _____

"A word fitly spoken is like apples of gold in settings of silver."

Proverbs 25:11

Conflict Resolution Solutions

Tips to Prevent and Resolve Conflict

VERONICA SITES

ISBN-10: 0-9975762-1-9
ISBN-13: 978-0-9975762-1-4

Dedication

Michael, Stephanie, Amy and my parents.
In the Lord, with your support and
encouragement I have flourished.
Thank you for being my champions.

Acknowledgments

My inexpressible gratitude to the awesome and amazing, longtime Administrative Assistant Ziglar Laurie Magers for excellence in editing and review.

Tom Ziglar, thank you for carrying out and extending the Zig Ziglar Legacy. Not only are you the proud son of Zig Ziglar, I am honored to call you "family."

Thank you Michelle Prince of Prince Performance Group.

To Chris D. Mendoza CAMM. arts LLC, Thank you for your tireless patience in creating art and cover design.

Foreword by Tom Ziglar

ZIGLAR HAS the privilege of including Veronica Sites among our Ziglar Legacy Certified trainers. She has been actively involved with ZLC for well over a year, and we are inspired by her obvious commitment and continuing growth.

I'm pleased that Veronica invited me to write the Foreword for *Conflict Resolution Solutions*. I truly can't think of many more relevant subjects for today's worldwide society. I can honestly say I don't remember when I've read a book that more succinctly expresses vital, workable answers to so many questions that touch on an area of such great need.

Veronica Sites draws from her extensive experience in the consulting and counseling fields to present the material in this book. I am confident any reader will benefit from this information and, if they apply it to their own relationships—personal, family, business or community—enjoy greater peace, harmony, and balance in their own life.

We at Ziglar are proud of the quality of our Ziglar Legacy Certified trainers. When people like Veronica Sites make valuable contributions to the needs of today's cultures, we are gratified to see them continuing the efforts initiated by my father, Zig Ziglar, nearly fifty years ago.

Introduction

THIS BOOK is the result of many interventions in careers and lessons learned personally.

Conflict is inevitable. How one chooses to navigate communication is a choice. We all communicate. However, considering results before we engage in a conversation may take a little time, yet is an investment well made. Preventing conflict leads more quickly to resolve and is less traumatic than careless words leading to a mess that can damage relationships rather than restore from dysfunction to healthy function.

With communication being such a fundamental part of getting along with others, it is insane to expect good results without skills. Is it any surprise communication is also one of the most neglected skill sets developed. Poor communication leads to conflict in all areas of life? Work, family, and inner conflict have become too common. Unresolved conflict is costly in society.

I wrote this book to meet a constant need for others: conflict resolution. Conflict is inevitable; effective communication is the key to preventing conflict before it starts. Many people experience conflict without knowledge of how it evolved, how to resolve it, or why it is almost predictable in certain scenarios.

You will find this practical for business and life. Whether one takes a job or gets married, the unrealistic expectation of thinking everyone will "just get along fine" or "work it out or just figure it out" just does not work. Companies and communities suffer from continued dysfunctional cycles of conflict and broken homes with little or no training of how to solve the communication problem. If you want resolve, you must make a choice to develop your skills to reach that goal. This is your tool.

This is my answer to conflict, be it at home, work, or inner conflict. I wrote this to help aim communication toward results, resolve, and peace with yourself. The only person you can directly improve is you. Sometimes inner conflict is a catalyst of poor performance, and negligible productivity. Use this book to be proactive and implement prevention, rather than serving in a constant state of intervention.

Education, prevention and intervention are critical.

We can learn something from everyone, be it what to do or what not to do, from someone else's failures. My mentor, Zig Ziglar, said, "Failure is an event, not a person." To that I say, "I will not let failure define me as a person. I will learn and make a difference."

Table Of Contents

Preparing

Tip 1
Know what conflict is

Webster defines conflict as a strong disagreement between people, groups, etc., that results in often angry argument: a difference that prevents agreement: disagreement between ideas, feelings, etc. Conflict happens the very instant a single expectation is unmet. It can be with others or personal inner conflict. Inner conflict takes place when we go against convictions, ethics, character, and counter to our personal values, and fall short of what we expect of ourselves. Are you conflicted?

Tip 2
Know conflict's dynamic

When an expectation is not met, responsive opinions form that may be either spoken or internalized and left unspoken or suppressed. These thoughts, feelings, or emotions lead to either actions or reactions.

Reactions are fueled by emotions. Responses are planned actions intended to lead to specific results. Think of a first responder. He plans, prepares, and responds at the right time. This is a guide to help you do the same.

Tip 3
Know the cause

Communication and misunderstanding are the primary causes of conflict. It can be the result of poor information, lack of information, misinformation, or simply no information. Consider that an expectation never expressed is communication never made. Good communication is the key to preventing conflict before it ever starts.

Tip 4
Build communication muscles

To minimize communication problems in business with clients and at home with family, the key is that you communicate clearly and in a timely manner. It is a good practice to have the listener say back to you what they understood you to say. This will help reduce the amount of uncertainty and avoid the majority of conflicts. Be careful; long periods of silence feed tension and undermine the security of a stable environment.

Tip 5
Know the target

Target results before tongues tangle in turmoil. It is easy to target a person and miss that the root of the problem is a behavior, attitude, or unmet expectation. Target the behavior and minimize the risk of generalities that can be internalized, break a spirit and result in invisible wounds.

Preventing Conflict

Tip 6
Take responsibility

Determine how you want to resume interaction following potential conflict. Do you
want continued tension or a peaceable
resolve?

You alone determine the course a conversation takes and the destination at which
you arrive: peace or chaos. Your actions
will follow the lead of your mindset and
plan. The tendency is that what you model negatively will be doubled by those
around you. What you do positively will
be carried out only half as much as it was
modeled.

Tip 7
Admit

Conflict may involve multiple people, yet there is one responsible party. Note that I did not say there is only one person responsible. Each individual person is responsible for controlling his thoughts, words, and actions. Admitting this can change the course of your conversation as much as it is within you to navigate around potential conflict.

Tip 8
Realize responsibility

Realizing responsibility takes action and a predetermined mindset. Taking responsibility is not about pointing blame. Responsibility is choosing to take action according to a desired result, rather than engaging on an emotional level and letting a conversation get out of control or become utter chaos.

Tip 9
Be realistic

Conflict is inevitable; how you handle it is completely up to you. You can only manage yourself. Do it in such a way that you can sleep peacefully at the end of the day. Know that you did what you could to communicate in a manner that you alone exercised control with intent to resolve rather than escalate a conversation. Whether it came about or not is not solely up to you. Take control of you and you sleep more peacefully. When you know you have done all you can to guide a conversation toward resolve, you must release control.

Tip 10
Recognize limitations

It is not within you to change someone else's thoughts, feelings, or the receptivity of the words exchanged in a conversation. It is very important to choose words that align with what is meant and what you mean the other person to understand you are saying. Words have meaning; speak with care and precision. No one likes to be misunderstood and everyone wants to be heard. Sometimes the words used are not in alignment with what is meant or understood.

Tip 11
Assess before you speak a word

Assess words before they are spoken. The impact words may have on a person contributes to the conversation or situation. Use words that build others up; encourage and edify when possible. There is something positive about the person with whom you speak. It may take forethought and intentionality to focus on the positives. Keep this in mind: sticks and stones can break bones, but words can crush one's spirit. Words can do more damage than what the eye will ever see. Choose not to cause invisible wounds. Ask yourself if what you are about to say is something you would benefit from if it were said to you.

Tip 12
Stop and Think

Think ahead. Choose to use words you would be 100% well in hearing if you were the recipient of your message. Remember, while passion and emotion may fuel word choice, you cannot retract what hits the airwaves. Once words leave the lips they reverberate in a time capsule of the mind and can create pain or stir deeply buried wounds that hit the heart, much like it feels to pick a tender scab. Curt words cannot be erased. The damage of thoughtless words destroys too many relationships.

Tip 13
Respect differences

In communication, individual personalities listen and communicate with major differences. By default this puts individuals at an advantage or disadvantage entering a conversation. Personality differences impact how many words are used to communicate a thought and how a person processes information received. Compound this with varied listening skills and you have a perspective that inevitably misses the mark of expectation differences. Some people use minimal words while others have verbal diarrhea when it comes to unloading information. This can be exhausting. Do you know your verbal listening style? Consider work in these areas.

Tip 14
Master the conversation

It is easier to master a conversation and develop effective communication skills than it is to resolve conflict. Prevention of poor or emotive communication is an intentional plan well executed with thought and results in mind.

Think of communication as a battle, and Conflict like war. Both require a peace treaty. It takes cool down time. Give yourself "time out" when emotions start to escalate.

Tip 15
Manage conflict

Conflict can be managed. In many cases, conflict is deterred or escalation minimized with an advanced, predetermined, desired result. With determination and planning, personal boundaries go a long way when it come to inner peace. A prepared person acts according to desired result. An unprepared person reacts and the conversation gets out of control. Emotions make bad choices. What is your desired result—chaos or self-control?

Tip 16
Stay the course

Determination and planning go a long way. When it comes to inner peace, a prepared person acts with results in mind. Start a conversation with the end in mind. How do you want the conversation to end?

Tip 17
Set boundaries

Determine boundaries for yourself concerning words and emotions. Will you choose to continue a conversation that triggers emotionally driven words? Or, will you choose (in advance) that at any point of personal escalation you will take a deep breath, choose to intently listen and communicate before you will resume your part of the conversation so that you will have time to calm down?

No one likes the thought of being on a highway with a drunk driver. They are all over the place without any consideration of others on the road. Pick the lane your conversation will operate from and drive

your speech accordingly. You cannot control the words others choose. Stay in your
lane, and arrive at your desired destination
safely.

Tip 18
Manage yourself

You are the only person you can control. You are only responsible for what you can manage and that is you. The conflict always involves you and someone or multiple others. Can you really control anyone else or their perception? (no) Communication can lead to sharing different perspectives. It cannot change a perception. If feelings tell the mind that "I" am being attacked verbally it is nearly impossible to convince the hearer of the words that their perception is not the case. In that case, feelings need time to calm down.

Tip 19
No blame game

Blame is counter-productive and takes no responsibility for one's words or actions. In order to disarm what may come across as a verbal attack rather than reaction with an immediate jump to defense, try the following clarifying sequence. "What I hear you saying is… Am I understanding you correctly?" After the answer if it is still unclear whether the verbiage was meant as an attack, follow up with: "I thought I heard… is that what is meant for me to take from this part of the conversation?" Using "I" statements takes the focus off the speaker and turns attention to the words and the intended message.

Tip 20
Choose battles carefully

The tendency in most people is to adopt an "I'm right, you are wrong" position or mentality. Engaging in conflict is a choice. If the potential conflict is between two people, both cannot be right, but both can be wrong in the way the conversation unfolds. Begin the conversation with the end in mind. Do you want resolve, or do you want escalated conflict and turmoil?

Tip 21
Guard your mind

Conflict involves others, whether a conversation is external or internal. Words
internalized along the way can impact
self-image, confidence, and contribute
to negative self-talk. Consider personal
mindset. The mind is like prime real estate.
It is your intellectual property; determine
in advance that you and your thoughts
have great value. Why give someone else
"squatters rights" to impact your thoughts,
fuel feelings, or have a "voice" in what you
retell yourself that others claim. Do you
want inner conflict?

Tip 22
Hold the line

Inner conflict is the result of forfeiting of healthy self-esteem, good confidence, and healthy self-image. Giving up mental real estate undermines a sense of security and fosters insecurity. Choose in advance what you will embrace in hearing and what you refuse to accept into the treasury of your thoughts and beliefs. What you give a place in your mind can either build up or be detrimental to one's emotional and mental health. Do you believe everything you hear?

Tip 23
Validate others

Validation serves in preventing escalation in communication. Everyone longs to be validated. A person's perspective is unique to them and filters through ears, mind, memories and internalized feelings. Hearing penetrates deeper than the surface of the mind. It is more than a single moment in a conversation. You are talking to a person who hears through a lifetime of history that may trigger feelings or, unbeknown to you, step on past hurts. Validating a person's feelings and value of perspective meets a need we all have. Validation can be as simple as saying "I had no idea." The act of listening validates. Do your feelings matter to you? Is your perspective important to you? The same is true for others.

Tip 24
Acknowledgment is not agreement

Acknowledgment communicates to others that their perspective has merit and value in the discussion. Acknowledgment sets the stage to guide a conversation toward resolve. You free yourself to hear as you listen when choosing to acknowledge that the person speaking wants to be heard as much as you expect and want to be heard.

Tip 25
Agree to disagree

Agreement yields quite a bit of power in preventing and keeping conflict from escalating. The power of agreement to disagree creates the opportunity for bickering parties to get away from staunch "I'm right and you are wrong" or "I don't care what you say, you are wrong" mentalities. The choice to agree to disagree is not a stalemate, it is a means of validation where each party acknowledges valid points where no progress is being made by continuing to argue. Agreement to disagree is a truce that takes action to resume the conversation in a productive direction. It allows a break or end to a conversation until everyone calms to a point that the conversation may resume civilly in an effort to reconcile a conflict.

Tip 26
Seize the power of silence

Silence speaks volumes. Sometimes just letting the person rattling on to decompress is the best thing for everyone. Refrain from interrupting, it often backfires. Interruptions communicate that what you have to say is more important than listening. Silence exercises self control. There is strength in meekness. Meekness is not weakness. It takes tremendous self control to silently listen. There may be no need or desire for a solution or further verbal engagement. Sometimes a person just wants to be heard. Listening validates the person and a perspective that matters to the one speaking. Wait to respond only if asked a question; even then, if it is a moment of rant, be sure to ask if the person actually wants an answer or suggestion for a solution. Do you like to be heard?

Tip 27
FIGHT!

Fight for positive results. Fight for the relationship not against each other as foes. Whether at work or at home, teamwork is individuals working toward a mutually beneficial goal. In the case of conflict, the goals should be resolve and stronger relationships.

Tip 28
Convince and convert.

Authentically be convinced that the relationship (work or personal) is worth preserving. The labor of working through miscommunication is worth working through your personal perspective to consider someone else's. It leads to resolve and converts into a profitable outcome.

Minimizing Conflict After It Starts

Tip 29
Distinguish fact from opinion

Know the difference between facts and opinions. Facts are unchanging and cannot be manipulated without denial or deception. False evidence can appear real if facts are not considered objectively. Opinions vary from person to person and can increase, depending on how many people are polled. Conflict tends to arise when opinions differ and escalate, based on subjective feelings that lead a person to think they are arguing based on facts alone. (see also tip 26)

Tip 30
Truth trumps facts

In card games like poker, the suit or run chosen to rank above others ends the game. This applies to choosing to prevent conflict escalation. The "truth trumps facts" principle determines ahead of time how a conversation will end in some form of resolve. The principle rightly used has the ability to prevent arguments with others and ourselves (more on this in the inner conflict section).

Keep it simple: facts are unchangeable and objective; opinions vary and are subjective—and dependent on changing variables.

Tip 31
Power of a trump

If someone tells another to "get over it," specifically concerning grief following a death, it will not end well. Consider these facts, opinions and truths. The fact is grief differs with the dynamic of a relationship. While one may continue crushed and struggling to move on with life, another may have emotionally progressed to a different place. The reason is that the re-lationship was initially different. No one should impose an opinion of a right way or amount of time to grieve.

A "trump" or truth sets boundaries con-cerning silence and needless conflict. In this case, the person expecting others to have "moved on or be over it" could insist on a right and wrong mindset, but, there is another option. The truth is that death and its survivors are in varying places emotionally.

Out of respect for the unique pain left by death, the trump principle takes into consideration that the more deeply connected a person was, the greater the need of respect and of the lifelong journey the survivor finds himself taking one step at a time.

Tip 32
Close communication gaps

The key to bridging communication gaps in business, with clients, or in a family, is to provide clear communication in a timely manner. There is a time and place for silence, but keep lines of communication open and current. This reduces uncertainty and risk of assumptions that can lead to anxiety and various emotions that contribute to conflicts.

Long periods of silence fuel tension and undermine a stable environment or situation. Where staff is concerned, silence can breed contention or undermine efforts of negotiation and resolution. Update on a regular basis when something is awry.

Fear of the unknown is common. Do not poke that proverbial bear; it can lead to a grizzly mess!

Tip 33
Know the process

For whatever reason, if an expectation is unmet, potential conflict is commonplace.

Sample scenario: An employee is told to close out the cash drawer. He does what he knows to do, but does it hurriedly, throwing all coins into the cash bag unaware that the reason each coin set goes into its own bag is for auditing purposes.

The next day the store is audited, points are deducted from the store's score, and that impacts his manager's pay.

Ultimately, there is need of a conversation and emotions may be high on one end, while the unsuspecting employee remains clueless that there is even a problem, let alone that it has escalated to a potentially volatile conversation. What do you do?

Tip 34
Be reasonable

Is it reasonable to impose expectations without communication, then get upset when expectations are unmet? Let me help you with the hard questions—no!

No one knows what they do not know. We all need intel and well-communicated expectations to achieve our goals and level of excellence.

Clear communication empowers a desired result.

Unspoken or unknown expectations lead to self-sabotaging a conversation, situation, relationship, and your own reasonable peace.

Tip 35
Be specific

Using generalities like "always" and "never" is similar to throwing gas on a fire. Rather than saying "you always…" use specific language with perspective and a current example.

Example: It may not seem this way to you, but to me it seems there is a high rate of not getting a task done and that leaves me confused by what is said and what does not get done.

Give an example such as, "When I ask for a task to be done and find it incomplete later, I am left to conclude something and I do. I become confused and frustrated, because the words did not match the actions. What would you like for me to conclude?" Note there are only first person pronouns in use.

Tip 36
Be in the moment

Keep the conversation current. Refrain from bringing up past or unresolved issues. Only when giving a specific example using the previous tips and pronoun focus of "I, me and my" perspective, should something from recent past come into the conversation.

Why? Examples help connect the principle with the behaviors or pattern being experienced.

Keep past arguments off limits to the current conversation.

Tip 37
Be 100% present

Few things communicate a lack of concern, interest, listening or focus more
often than interruptions that turn attention to an electronic device. Each
conversation is important. Turn off and do
not bring technology to talk time. Turning
attention away from conflict communicates many things non-verbally, whether
intended or not. Texting, checking mes-
sages, even glancing at a vibrating phone,
communicates that there is something
more important than respecting the person in front of you enough to be heard
when it is your turn.

Tip 38
Know your policy

An organization's size should not determine the need to have documented policies. A policy is not a procedure nor is a procedure a policy. Policy clarifies protocol and is for operational reference. Policies are relevant when concerns or accusations of leniency transpire.

For a business owner, policy provides boundaries, operational guidelines, and empowers objectivity.

Example: A long-time employee asks what is not customary concerning his date of retirement. He has earned a bonus and company policy states that that employee would forfeit all bonuses earned unless remaining employed and working the very payday that bonuses are paid. Policy says no; however, the owner can advise how to navigate within acceptable procedure to accomplish the retiree's and company's goal. Policy encourages integrity.

Tip 39
Understand procedure

Procedures navigate operations within policy. Procedures do not trump policy, but are the operational steps of carrying out policies.

Example: The corporation of a franchise requires an "internal DBA." A franchise coach follows procedure, consulting between the franchisee and marketing department. They arrive at a deadlock concerning "DBA" name. Everything followed procedure without consideration of policy. Knowing the value of policy, the franchisee asked a pivotal question that changed the direction from opinions given to conclude with the task accomplished. With no policy preventing the franchisee from choosing the preferred "DBA," policy, procedures, systems and operation worked in tandem to arrive at a solution. Valuing policy and procedure can often expedite an end to conflict. In this case, the company recognized a need to clarify "DBA naming" guidelines. Without guidelines (policy), sometimes conflict drags on too long.

Change
and Inner
Conflict

Tip 40
Change the perspective

Change is a part of life. Sometimes we want change, and embracing it is voluntary. Other times it can crash in like an unwelcome intruder. In that case, what is "normal" up to that moment is scattered in a million directions, leaving us broken in the wake. You have two options: bristle in resistance and battle it, or see it as unexpected opportunities. One of the greatest opportunities is to co-create a new normal. The best news is that with learning and unlearning, your new normal can lead you to a transformed life.

Tip 41
Know normal

Normal varies from one person to the next. Avoid comparing someone else's normal to your own. What may seem normal on the surface because of a person's functionality, despite what is unknown, may be far from anything you would ever want to call normal in anyone's life. It took a long time for that person to arrive at their normal. It is best to know what is normal for you and work toward growth from there.

Tip 42
No normal

When any normal is interrupted be aware that it is common to incite intense emotions and feelings like fear, anger, frustration, numbness, loss or perhaps like you are in a fog or slow motion. Sometimes a person is not able to feel at all; this is shock. The effect and reaction to an interruption to normal is in direct proportion to the traumatic impact it makes, starting the moment of interruption to what normal was. No normal is not the worst place to be. It is actually a place of great possibility, because it will likely require rebuilding to establish a new normal.

Tip 43
Let it go

Worry predicts an outcome and camps out there. What you focus on grows in intensity and, before long, it creates a bonfire of thoughts that soon blaze out of control like a wildfire of conjecture. You add no value to any circumstance by worrying. Worry impacts stress levels starting with you and rippling out to others. It affects your physical, mental, and emotional health. A single moment has enough to focus on to make the choices necessary to improve a situation rather than anxiously predicting an error.

WE DON'T think about it, but at any given moment we are in a phase of life where thoughts, feelings, actions, and results are concerned. The following tips are to guide you with thoughts of the result you may really want. It is challenging to maintain a sober mind flooded by emotions, clouded by chaotic or negative thoughts. The phases we navigate through include survival, stability, success, and significance. Theses final tips are my sweet spot. I cannot express enough how inner conflict was conquered navigating and implementing these powerful tips.

Tip 44
Evaluate your situation

It is important to realize that you are unique. When you encounter a change or conflict others have faced, you bring to the situation everything unique to you. Consider that you are who you and where you are because of what has gone through your mind.

You are designed like no one else to accomplish and navigate what no one else can.

You have the ability to co-create the change you desire.

Tip 45
Anchor your mindset

In crisis, conflict, or a time of change there are some things that are very normal, because you are human. Psychologist call it "fight, flight, freeze or fawn." Since I help many people who deal with PTSD I want to make the distinction that PTSD is hyper arousal that is an acute stress response and physiological reaction that occurs in response to a perceived harm or threat to survival. Have you been there?

An anchor is a moment of extreme focus, where you declare intent and muster courage to face that you are in a storm. You recognize that this storm will pass. You breathe in possibility and exhale the shock, pain or numbness that lets you

know the worst is over and you must chart
a course to a better place or phase of life.

Tip 46
Assess what remains

In an F5 tornado, nothing remains standing. It is hard to take it all in as a responder, even more so as a survivor. I chose this imagery because sometimes what is faced internally feels likes the damage of what an F5 tornado leaves outwardly, only it is not visible and these are burdens of silent suffering people may be carrying.

Invisible wounds are critical, and only you know the depth and impact of such an inner conflict. You are engineered for success, designed to succeed, and possess the greatness of potential, whether you feel it or not. You must make up your mind to let someone know you need help, direction, and answers for how to navigate forward in the best possible way.

It takes the courage and strength of a warrior to ask for help. Do it!

Tip 47
Take ownership

Nothing belongs to you until you decide to embrace, accept, and receive it. Change comes with opportunity. You determine the extent of realizing the potential of bettering yourself, life and circumstances. When you own the opportunity, the possibility of co-creating a new chapter of life, comes through growth and as a result of current "survival decisions."

Tip 48
THRIVE

Change starts in a survival mode during the survival phase. Some say that the first is the worst when it comes to living in a survival mode. I agree. It is only a phase to be visited, but do not plan to stay. Living in survival mode can exhaust and create a wearisome lifestyle, lacking peace, joy, and satisfaction. It is natural to experience fear, anxiety, feelings of insecurity, an identity crisis, and uncertain or damaged self-esteem. You might find yourself asking, "Who am I or how did this happen?" Survival is a passing phase.

Focus on navigating to stability with a final destination of significance. If you are not familiar with setting goals for achievement, hire a coach. Be teachable, and seek to learn as much as unlearn everything necessary to thrive. Life is short: embrace it to the fullest.

Tip 49
Set goals

In the stability phase, you are like a ship. You may be tattered, worn, and have taken in a lot of water so that the situation seems like you could drown. Perhaps your dreams were shattered and trust ripped apart, but your sails will catch wind to set sail again. You have hope, and it is a strong anchor steadying a determined mindset. You must purpose to navigate and arrive at a better place: significance.

Your journey from survival to stability is weathering winds of change. With each crashing wave of accomplishment, confidence is gained and you experience a newly-found sense of security. You may be challenged to determine what success is to you, and on your way to success, which is only phase three, many have been lost at sea, never finding the safe harbor of the better life desired. How will you know you have arrived? Will others tell you? Will it be a balance in a bank account or a certain lifestyle? Will it include peace? Only you can determine your success. I can assure you your life is significant and where you are on the journey has significance.

Tip 50
Define success

While we all long to succeed, know that success is subjective and one man's success may be another's rung in the proverbial ladder of success. True and profound success includes happiness, peace, joy, freedom, a healthy peace of mind, body, and spirit.

Success should not suck the life out of you. If you find yourself there, remember safe harbor is found at the greatest destination: significance. Press onward, surround yourself with "like values" people that share the same moral compass and unwavering values. Like minded people on a journey are great, but when you live your life according to someone else's definition of success, you may be distracted from reaching phase four and the ultimate destination of significance.

Are you searching for purpose?

Tip 51
Live significantly

Significance is not an illusive harbor or vanishing point on the horizon. It is where purpose is found. It is where a hindsight view and perspective of all you have traveled to get "there" become priceless landmarks of your significant journey. Everything you have encountered on the journey of change is instrumental to who you are and where you are now. You are here. You are no longer there (in the past). You are here and now is your time to thrive. God never wastes a hurt. Significance is where freedom is found; you are free to impact others without concern of popular demand.

Winning
in Life

Tip 52
Share the wealth

Things that touch our lives are significant and serve a greater purpose when we allow our growth to encourage and empower others on their journey. You are living, indisputable proof that your story and achievements matter. Someone needs all that you have to offer. No one will be more effective at impacting a life in similar circumstances to what you have experienced the way that you can. It is time to live a life of giving. There you will find joy and satisfaction in knowing that you are fulfilling your purpose. Your purpose is to give others hope.

Tip 53
Be bold

Inner conflict is possible in anyone's life. Ironically an inner conflict can often be spotted most easily or with familiarity by someone who has experienced similar invisible wounds. My mom often told me "you can spot it when you've got it." Familiarity comes with insight. You will have and see countless opportunities if you just look around. Be bold, someone feeling weak or defeated needs your confidence and hope with evidence of what they can achieve too. Speak words of life. The verbal hope offer is backed by the evidence of your life that "they too" can overcome any conflict be it external or internal.

Tip 54
Be brave

Sometimes conflicted lives or situations need the bravery of others to find a way out of unspeakable situations. Muster courage to be a source of empowerment. Unresolved conflict can result in captivity. No one wants to be held captive to doubt, fear, anxiety, or worse in cases of abuse. Be brave to the extent that you take action and do not wait for someone else to do something.

Tip 55
Be an advocate

Everyone at some time needs an advocate. Today, schools teach anti-bullying. It is as imperative that adults not miss out on learning about bullying. Bully behavior is cruel, hurtful, not true, demeaning, degrading, negative, harsh, and causes invisible wounds that crush the spirit. If your self talk is at all like this, it is no less destructive than that of a bully. The problem is a bullying case of stinking thinking. You need to advocate for you! Stand up for yourself. Stop the trash talk. Be an advocate to yourself and seek to build others up too. Do for yourself what might come easier to do for others.

It is not arrogant to care for yourself.

Tip 56
Champion others

When you are moved or bothered by an unmet need, be the solution. When it comes to conflict, the only way anyone wins is when the wiser, more capable person, champions the cause of some else's betterment. Conflict resolution does not always mean agreement; it moves past the conflict championed by valuing others.

Tip 57
Live Free

It is liberating to know that the conflicts and struggles we encounter can and actually do serve to help others. Learning to resolve conflict is a paradigm shift that breaks the cycle of hurt people hurting people. Choosing to grow in areas of deficiency resets behavioral patterns. It establishes new habits with the benefit of becoming "free." The beauty of maturing and growth in freedom of damaging cycles is that people free, free people! Unresolved conflict is a prison, whether it is conflict with others or inner conflict. Ultimately, unresolved conflict boils down to how individuals manage inner conflict. The choice is yours.

Conclusion

IMPLEMENTING THESE tips has great rewards. Resolve takes diligence and determination. I believe you will find the investment of time and effort to result in the wonderful great reward of healthy relationships. I have seen these tips practiced lead to preserving jobs, friendships, and even marriages. Good communication is the key to productive conversations. Good communication is the key to prevent conflict before it ever starts. Use this as a guide to preventing conflict before it ever starts.

About The Author

Veronica Sites is a great speaker, proficient in English and Spanish. She provides practical content with proven results. She is an excellent communicator with strong skill in conflict resolution. She is a life student of studying the dynamic of conflict with others and personal inner conflict to offer practical solutions. Excellence in communication and listening gained recognition by FEMA and Victim Relief Ministry leadership during chaplaincy service following the tragic events of Hurricane Katrina. Her professional decorum and diplomacy led to being commissioned to contribute to disaster response manuals for how to effectively work though worst-case scenarios in a death notification.

She is a model of effective communication and listening. Her impact spans conflict in work environments, family crisis, and personal or inner conflict. Her message is packed with the conviction that everyone longs to be valued and respected. She understands that personality dynamics and past experiences impact how people can best resolve conflict. She implements communication skills, psychology, and personality assessment proficiency to shed light on how emotional and intelligent qutients all factor into human interaction. Among her credentials are certifications as speaker, trainer, and coach by the Ziglar Inc., and Critical Incident Stress Management. She is a dynamic people magnet!

Her heart for people and their betterment is no secret. She was awarded Chaplain of the year 2003, for SLI McDonalds, Inc., in Dallas, Texas. Personal development is her heartbeat and helping others is her mission.

Website
www.conflictresolutionspeaker.com

Social Media
https://www.facebook.com/conflictresolutionspeaker
https://www.linkedin.com/in/veronicasites
https://twitter.com/VeronicaSites

Motivation
Inspiration
Transformation
Conflict Resolution

VERONICA SITES welcomes the opportunity to inspire the audience at your next event. As contributing author featured in *Dare To Be A Difference Maker*, vol. 4, and author of *Rachael Did You Know*,

and *Fearless Faith*, she continues to write books that impact lives and inspire hope and help where it is needed most. Her expertise spans business, mentorship, coaching and public speaking. She is fluently bilingual in Spanish and connects with audiences all over the world.

Why you should book Veronica

• Powerful

Her story is a powerful testament of a life transformed and personal development. You will be inspired, motivated and challenged to take action. Her message delivers indisputable evidence of being a true difference maker.

• Authentic

Integrity is the cornerstone of who she is and how she serves others. She consistently lives out her mission: to impact community one life at a time.

• Dedicated

With transparent professionalism and alignment with Ziglar Legacy performance, you can expect motivation delivered with the focus on serving, "You can have everything in life you want, if you just help enough others get what they want."

• Committed

Her greatest goal is to make sure your event is an absolute success.

• Unique

Edutainment is an educational method of engaging an audience with some entertaining wow factor that keeps them remembering you for a long time.

The Ideal Speaker for:

- Business Meetings
- Schools, Colleges, University
- Churches
- Women's Groups & Organizations
- Conferences / Retreats
- Break out Sessions

Speaking Topics

- Goal Setting & Achievement
- Building Winning Relationships
- Communication That Works
- Unleashing Potential
- Becoming a Top Performer

- Fearless Faith
- Overcoming Traumatic Transitions
- Care for Caregivers
- Military to Marketplace
- Transition From Military to Civilian Life

BOOK NOW!

Contact Availability
book@ConflictResolutionSpeaker.com

Veronica Sites Speaker / Coach
ConflictResolutionSpeaker.com

www.ingramcontent.com/pod-product-compliance
Lightning Source LLC
Chambersburg PA
CBHW050539280326
41933CB00011B/1646